The peace in these hills and valleys is a peace that unravels the knitted brow and quiets the nerves of the hand; it restores in us a zest for life.

This collection of photographs has been selected carefully to represent the variety of sites to be seen and will help you to enjoy, again and again, the mysterious beauty of the Great Smoky Mountains National Park.

front cover: Great Smoky Mountains National Park from the Blue Ridge Parkway
right: Oliver Cabin, Cades Cove
following pages: Entrance to Cades Cove

A full color Photographic Tour of the

great smoky mou

America's most popular National Park

From the photographs of:
Jim Doane, John Earl, Larry Harwell,
Walter Kennedy and James Roddy
Published by
Aerial Photography Services, Inc.
2300 Dunavant Street
Charlotte, North Carolina 28203
© 1981 Aerial Photography Services, Inc.
full color litography by KINA Italia, Sp.A., Milan, Italy
First Edition April 1981
Library of Congress Catalog Card Number 81-65809

ains

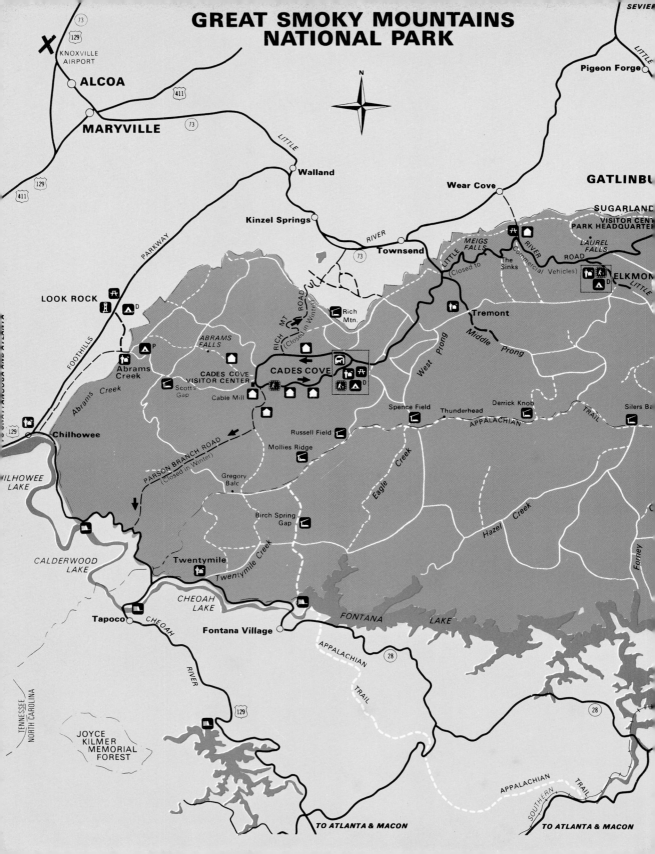

GREAT SMOKY MOUNTAINS NATIONAL PARK

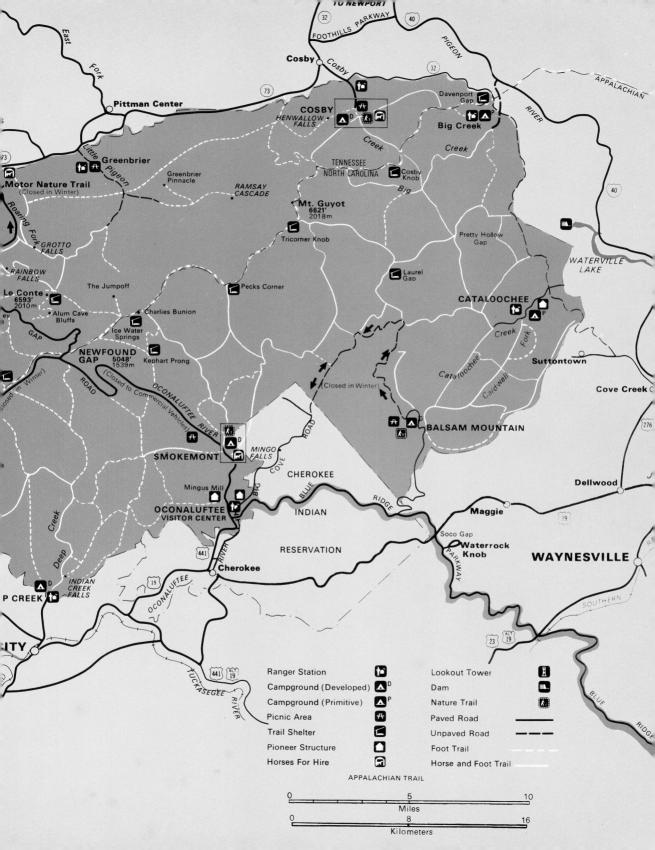

TO NEWPORT

FOOTHILLS PARKWAY

Cosby

Cosby

PIGEON

APPALACHIAN

RIVER

Pittman Center

East
Fork

COSBY
HENWALLOW
FALLS

Davenport
Gap

Big Creek

Creek

Greenbrier

Little
Pigeon

Greenbrier
Pinnacle

Creek

TENNESSEE
NORTH CAROLINA

Cosby
Knob

Big

Motor Nature Trail
(Closed in Winter)

RAMSAY
CASCADE

Mt. Guyot
6621'
2018m

Pretty Hollow
Gap

WATERVILLE
LAKE

GROTTO
FALLS

Tricorner Knob

Roaring Fork

RAINBOW
FALLS

The Jumpoff

Pecks Corner

Laurel
Gap

CATALOOCHEE

Le Conte
6593'
2010m

Alum Cave
Bluffs

Charlies Bunion

Ice Water
Springs

Creek

Fork

Suttontown

GAP

NEWFOUND
GAP
5048'
1539m

Kephart Prong

(Closed to Commercial Vehicles)

OCONALUFTEE RIVER

ROAD

(Closed in Winter)

BALSAM MOUNTAIN

Cove Creek

276

Cataloochee

Cardwell

(Closed in Winter)

SMOKEMONT

MINGO
FALLS

COVE

ROAD

BLUE

CHEROKEE

Dellwood

Mingus Mill

OCONALUFTEE
VISITOR CENTER

INDIAN

RIDGE

Maggie

19

RESERVATION

Soco Gap

PARKWAY

Waterrock
Knob

WAYNESVILLE

Creek

Deep

441

RIVER

Cherokee

19

INDIAN
CREEK
FALLS

P CREEK

SOUTHERN

ITY

OCONALUFTEE

19
ALT

23
19
ALT

BLUE

TUCKASEGEE
RIVER

441

19
ALT

RIDGE

Ranger Station		Lookout Tower	
Campground (Developed)	D	Dam	
Campground (Primitive)	P	Nature Trail	
Picnic Area		Paved Road	
Trail Shelter		Unpaved Road	
Pioneer Structure		Foot Trail	
Horses For Hire		Horse and Foot Trail	

APPALACHIAN TRAIL

0   5   10
Miles

0   8   16
Kilometers

Great Smoky Mountains National Park

The most popular National Park in America is a territory of 800 square miles, about 60 miles in length and 20 miles in width that straddles the west border of North Carolina and the east border of Tennessee. It is a magnificent location of Vacation Land for the crowded East of our Nation.

Geologists tell us that over two hundred million years ago, there was a great upheaval of the Earth's surface in this Appalachian area and the Great Smoky Mountains were formed from a shallow sea. For these millions of years, erosion of water and wind did its work. Valleys and slopes which exist today were formed — and now we have 16 peaks over 6,000 feet and 53 over 5,000 feet in height. The valleys range from a low point of 857 feet at Abrams Creek on the west and ascends in a broken array of valleys and peaks to a height of 6,642 feet at Clingmans Dome, the highest mountain in the park. All this forms a panorama of beauty. Within its borders you will find deep gorges, gentle slopes, rapid streams, clear pools, jagged rocks, great forests and rich meadows.

Plant life is in profusion. You will find 1,300 kinds of flowering shrubs and plants, 130 different kinds of trees, nearly 30 varieties of orchids and grasses of all kinds. Nourished by a rich soil, a heavy rainfall (about 80 inches), and the sun of our most temperate zone makes the area of this Park one of the most luxuriant of the World — the Kashmir, the Shangri-La of America.

The profuse growth of vegetation (being close packed Rhododendron and Mountain Laurel) combines with the oil of the pines to exude an aroma and a vapor that rises and mixes with the feathery fleece of the fog. It clings to the top of the mountains and sinks to the valleys below — and you have the Smokies, and the reason for the name — The Great Smoky Mountains National Park.

Let us tell you how the Smokies became one of our National Parks. As you may know, most all of our other parks were set aside from government lands and before the private individual could claim any ownership. However, with the Smokies it was different. For years its land was owned by private individuals and lumber companies as it contained one of the finest spreads of lumber in the United States. Spruce, fir and hemlock — oak, walnut and other fine woods grew straight and tall. Then came the devastating forces of man. Private enterprise in the form of saw mills began to destroy one of the most beautiful wilderness areas of the nation.

Fortunately, one of the reasons we are a great nation and people is that in time of need there always has been an individual who has come to our rescue. In this case, Mrs. Willis P. Davis of Knoxville, Tennessee, who realized the grandeur of the area, started a movement to change the entire complex to a National Park.

Others followed — and John D. Rockefeller, Jr. contributed $ 5,000,000. This amount was added to funds from State, Federal and private sources and the lands of the Smokies was purchased and given to the Federal Government. On September 8, 1940, the Great Smoky Mountains National Park became a reality when it was formally dedicated by President Franklin D. Roosevelt.

by John Locke

following pages: Gatlinburg, Tennessee at the entrance to the Great Smoky Mountains National Park.

Gatlinburg, Tennessee
top left: The Sky Lift
top right: Looking south towards
Mt. Le Conte
right: Looking east from the By-pass

The entrance to the Great Smoky Mountains
National Park near Gatlinburg

GREAT SMOKY
MOUNTAINS
NATIONAL PARK

UNITED STATES DEPARTMENT OF THE INTERIOR
NATIONAL PARK SERVICE

top: Visitor Center Park Headquarters
at Sugarlands
right: Little River at the entrance to the Park

Mt. Guyot 6621' (2018 m)

right: Le Conte Lodge, availabl
only on foot, and Mt. Le Cont

Mt. Mitchell 6684' (2037 m)

Conte 6593' (2010 m)

top left: Alun Cave Bluffs;
top right: Charlies Bunion;
botton left: Rainbow Falls;
botton right: The Old Mill on background;
right: Grotto Falls.

The Appalachian Trail enters the Park at Fontana and Davenport Gap, crossing about 88 miles of the Great Smoky Mountains National Park.

top left: Sunset near Charlies Bunion;
top righ: Heath Balds in the southwest section of the park;

bottom left: one of the bear-proof trail shelters;
bottom right: a trail marker.

ft: The Chimney Tops along the Little
geon River
ove: Ramsay Cascade

following pages: A magnificent sunset
from Clingmans Dome

Clingmans Dome 6642' (2025 m),
the highest mountain in the Park

top: A sunset seen from the roadway at Newfound Gap,
bottom: The parking area at Newfound Gap and a glimpse of Highway 441 winding its way through the Park.
at left: The crisp white lovliness of a winter snow adds a special magic to Newfound Gap 5048' (1539 m)

following pages: south of Newfound Gap on the Skyway, looking to the west

Kanati Fork on the Oconaluftee River

top: Scenic U.S. 441 forms this exciting loop as it climbs from Gatlinburg to 5048' (1539 m) at Newfound Gap,
bottom: an overlook along Transmountain Highway 441 shows one of the multitude of breathtaking views discovered at virtually every bend

In springtime, the Park
returns to new life and is
resplendent with dogwood
blooms from middle
to late April.

The roadways in the Park take on a special
brilliance in autumn, a favorite time for visitors.
left: The Great Smoky Mountains National Park
seen from the Blue Ridge Parkway near
Cherokee, North Carolina.

Top: Coming down the Skyway toward Cherokee,
North Carolina,
Bottom: Mingus Mill near Cherokee

Indian Creek Falls near Bryson City

Aunt Winchester, matriarch of the Smokies. This painting of the resident of the Great Smoky Mountains at the age of 100 years is hanging in the Oconaluftee Visitor Center.

At the southern entrance to the Great Smoky Mountains National Park, this Ranger Station and Pioneer Museum displays pioneer artifacts covering nearly two centuries of life in the Southern Highlands.

t the entrance to the Great Smoky
ountains National Park near Cherokee,
orth Carolina.

elow: The Blue Ridge Parkway joining U.S.
1 near the Oconaluftee Visitor Center

The Qualla Cherokee Indian Reservation
joins the Great Smoky Mountains National
Park at the southern entrance.
It is the home of the Eastern band of the
Cherokee Indians, many of whom were forced
to Oklahoma on the infamous
"Trail of Tears" march.

The Oconaluftee Indian Village depicts
the Cherokee way of life where you can see
an interesting study of the past, as well as see
the handwork and crafts of the Cherokee.